Advance Praise for *Enter the Water*

'A dark-light beauty'
Ali Smith

'*Enter the Water* has horizons and wit and allusion and rhyme
and disenchanted politics and birds, and lines that hit the reader
right in the heart. The emotional depth and intellectual scope are
extraordinary. The writing is original and perfectly pitched, the
developing narrative shares an anger at the uncaring corruption of the
world with an awareness that being a person means "it is lonely
being at the centre of things". A significant debut'
Ian Patterson

'Totally compelling, *Enter the Water* pulls you along like a
current. Gentle, deft, spacious yet searingly vivid, it wanders like
our narrator and shows us both nature and the city through new eyes.
With razor sharp questions and keen observations, our systems of
power and privilege are destabilised and the precarity of existing in
the current moment is exposed. This is a book full up to the throat
with feeling; the intensity and inexpressibility of love, of uncertainty
and displacement. But it's also funny, wry and original. This book will
sneak up on you and leave its music long ringing in your ears'
Cecilia Knapp

'Eviction, insomnia, techno-divination and mythologies that
"begin with a bird" mark the psychic "circumference" of *Enter the
Water*. This is "a narrative of trying" performed or lived as a book of
poetry. Gates open unexpectedly, startling both the person exiting
a space and the one peering in. It's this quality of being "both in and
out always" that I most appreciate about Jack Wiltshire's writing. It's
a place that's both visceral and perceptive, a discomfort formulated
in great tenderness and pain. All the water in the book, all the
animals and insects and birds: help. How "the felt-tip green of a
butterfly" is a form of titration: a way to follow something,
to look up, to stay connected, until it disappears'
Bhanu Kapil

ENTER THE WATER

JACK WILTSHIRE

corsair poetry

C O R S A I R

First published in the UK in 2023 by Corsair

1 3 5 7 9 10 8 6 4 2

A CIP catalogue record for this book
is available from the British Library.

ISBN: 978-1-4721-5818-5

Typeset in Perpetua by M Rules Ltd
Printed and bound in Great Britain by
Clays Ltd, Elcograf S.p.A.

Papers used by Corsair are from well-managed forests
and other responsible sources.

Corsair
An imprint of
Little, Brown Book Group
Carmelite House
50 Victoria Embankment
London EC4Y 0DZ

An Hachette UK Company
www.hachette.co.uk

www.littlebrown.co.uk

. . . wailing gulls blew in from the sea across the freshly ploughed fields,
but Marianne had never seen the sea

Heroes and Villains,
ANGELA CARTER

Tell all the Truth but tell it slant

'1129',

EMILY DICKINSON

finish

I

he's not always a nice guy, Nature
but he tells me   he's all i've got

—

how does it keep growing in the same spot
and is that what really makes the flower?

—

a van coughs down a driveway
idle, i watch
some unsatisfied tourists
dithering about the wet steps of a fountain

there's a crack in me
where the coins slip in,
i've been ridden my entire life
like the pay-slot pony at Asda

i neigh
in mechanical amusement

—

another day
Nature's yet to pay me a visit of leaves on my windowsill

i'm waiting
and i'm wanting

i'm not asking for much, there's an alleyful below
but none here so i'm feeling low

here he is, he laughs
you're still living in a flat, you mongrel?

Priti Patel plans to sonic BOOM refugees crossing the channel, says
the news on my phone

god they really hit, don't they?
they do, says Nature
those Sambuca shots we're downing

i'm not happy with this place, i want to move
oh? says Nature
but i have nowhere else to go
oh?

so blue
the room spins in waves

another round? Nature offers

—

my hump's stuck in the eye of a needle
the end jabbed in my eye

7

today i'm a deer, Muntjac specifically
i've 'woke' up thinking about how language had me
in multiple positions from the beginning
more than i've liked

—

there's a shifty pigeon on the building across from me
there's six
did you know they bow and flick their tail up when they want a shag?
i've always just stood on the bridge at Trinity, arse curved like an
arc-light
the porters would   hum by my misery

i can't decide
whether i like
this view
of blue tarpaulin
along the roofs
or the bulk of bird
shit, a bit
mulberry-blue,
nor you
who
always look
down at night
not up
at that
not so blithe
ball of white
nor at
my indent
in a wall,
this flat
that
me and the pigeons
lean
    into

i frightened a lady
when i opened a side gate to my university;
she was trying to see through a gap in the door

'oh my! i didn't expect it to open
oh! that was so funny'

i looked at her and smiled
continued walking

she hadn't imagined a door could open
in this city

—

gel of a blackbird's eye, slime around its turning rim
as it slides for the plastic bag, for the Quorn behind the packaging

Ghosh writes about writers mining their own personal experiences for their work, their tremendous labour birthing what is essentially just another rehashed jumble of the same old words of the same old propaganda containers, then titles his book *The Great Derangement* so what the fuck am i supposed to think?
i think you're supposed to dig, says Nature
i think i wish my arsehole wasn't an excavation site since the age of gosh
you're not very good at looking after yourself, says Nature

—

there's no HERO story to this narrative, no line it'll follow to ensure it'll exalt you from the rest of the crowd of the same old containers of the same old culture of evasion

fuck me

littered underneath the carpet were the bodies of bugs
this left me feeling restless because
what's buried remains

to have a mind like
the sky
all that's part of life
unlike
the scrying glass
that is the television

i pick the television up
i shuffle the blackbird aside
throw the screen
outside and
sit the blackbird
in its place

—

there's really nowhere else to sit
in my flat that's
not that flat
but crooked;
i'm wedged between all
these
craggy surfaces

if there's not an envelope full of leaves waiting on the ragged mat of
my flat when i get back from town, i'm going to burn this shithole
down

—

there's not a single leaf
but there are pages containing an eviction notice
for a name i'm refusing at the moment

i lie down
on the grass by a park bench
thinking of a bench my pal mentioned to me in Chania
where she sat with her head on a backpack catnapping
i have no backpack   i couldn't even open successfully a carton of
eggs
i talk in my sleep
yet i like the blue tint placarding the trees with the sobby status of
my futurism
i like the wind
i like the fact that i have reached and dragged from the nearby bushes
all the leaves i could manage and built myself an empire to parallel
that of god in the sky

II

if i were to dream up a mythology
it would not begin with a guy piling leaves into a mound
it would begin with a bird

i'm interested in contemplating origins
and their bearings upon the present
but i would not wish
for anything so absolute as an ending

imagine a bird in a nest
a hand rising from the earth

it drags the cold bird down
believing it to have been starving

the warm hand of the earth holds all of the little bird
except for the seed slipping from its beak

once released, the bird returns to find another tree and spring
up comes another set of wings

casually the first bird searches in the undergrowth
for another seed

for a way back into the fretful earth
soon, an endless line of birds

each with a single seed
except for the first bird

it must leave the forest

what on earth
or who
decides the roots you
place, who
uproots the roots
you place, especially
in an institution with
roots deeper than
any individual, than
any light has ever
reached? who is it
that denies
the home you
make, every breath you
take, who decides who
can curb your space
your airways
your voice?
is it
you?

the pigeons are living in the tree above my bench
the council has spent thousands on defensive strategies
to defend against   rough sleeping
i have my own defensive strategies
i stay on the circumference
of the bench   of sleep
i have my own planetary bodies orbiting me
those shifty pigeons with sapphire rings in their eyes
they follow me

—

the pigeon
shit
   rains
like Tory rhetoric
avoid it
          avoid it
avoid it
they're sitting pretty
in their safe space, on their sacred branch

stars squint at the night sky
i guess the law isn't something they have to live by

i watch the stars waltz
they were once thought to be holes
through which one could catch a glimpse of heaven

our faith in the stability of the stars remained unshaken
until 1572, our faith that everything in this universe
has its right place
is no more

no more our faith in the fixedness of us
in class?

i stare out to the stars
my dreams of other worlds pass by

then i move
for love

'to their surprise, they found pronounced dips in light corresponding
to 65 evenly spaced clouds of planetary debris orbiting the star every
25 hours'
there's been a discovery
'in the habitable zone'
a celebration of possibility
for the scientists
but not for the homeless chap
covering himself in a pile of leaves

i think i'll only ever be the animal that sips sap
out of the life-tree,
i say to the chap with the handcuffs

i'm in the cell of a prison
that'll fuck the me right out of astronomy

there's a potted plant
and a potted me and many
many identical ceilings

—

from it i eat a leaf
then convulse
cellulose is a hard material to digest
cellulose requires specialist enzymes that
evolution has not designed for us

i convulsed on the circumference of a bottle of chardonnay
imported by Myliko International Wines
the day i was supposed to graduate
i liked it

u lose, says Nature, tormenting me

i feel my pulse
replace it
with a mystery

—

i had to demonstrate
a narrative of trying

according to the committee that decided if i passed my degree

i had to provide proof of work
rather than work on coping

some great vampiric monstrosity
living by consuming the dumb-blood
the shared sea-pulse writhing through this city

the blackbird taps the window of my cell
the pigeons gift me scraps from the outside

—

from the outside i weave my bed of sticks
they have blessed me
Valentines and the birds are signalling again
despite the pricks
cutting down their homes

—

i watch whoever it is that sits outside on a bench at night
they might be watching the stars
        or secretly underpinning all of society through a great
thunderclapping tut
as a pigeon steals their bread roll

Nature's head bobs up
and down at the window
i'm back! he says
with a gobful of Chinese takeaway
noodle?
nob off you tit, i say
his burps are a bird call
no receiver

what do you want? i ask
how will you pay the rent?
i don't want to write about this
take a leaf out of my book, says Nature
to put it simply, sex pays
says Nature

—

there's a disease at the core of us all
and it's not the one that shares its name with a beer
so we all cheer throw our arms up in the air
just don't care that we've got it
we just don't care

the chap with the handcuffs walks in while i'm getting my oil
changed by the blackbird
'err   who's that?' he points to Nature
who's stood outside salivating
with tar pools in his eyes
a sly curvature of the mouth

could you please give us a moment? i ask
'err   yeah sure'
thanks, i say as he leaves the room

a gelatinous wink from the blackbird

for a gene to push itself through a population, the individual has to
1) not die
2) reproduce
and even then it has a chance of dropping off

—

i lie down
on the carpet of a courtroom
i do not drop off   to sleep

i am used to the law
it has a history in my family between blackbird
and battery

i stole a leaf as i walked in
held it between my teeth and rolling tongue

i can see someone recording the court hearing
and a jury of pigeons who bow row after row
they wait for my signal

—

there is the shift of a pigeon's foot
i take this to be the opposite of the improbable
explainable in a way that all other things become
i take this to be another gift
me and my bodies and this ring of habits i cannot see without a
telescope because i'm short-sighted, i shift —
me and the camera fixed
on the black-mass cloud of limbs and beaks pecking

do you do anything sporty? asks Nature
i run
that's not sporty is it, you don't play running, there's no team
still running

—

until i lie down
under a bypass spray-painted with a sea-scene
in the middle of the city
i lie down
and a wing lands by me, tucks in its bedsheet-feathers
and for the last time   today
i'll lie down
until i become nothing but the horizon line

III

writing has a point
it's needle-like

how it shines
how it threads
into a magpie's nest

—

there's softer ground under the concrete i sleep on
there's soil, somehow

—

she appears but she might as well be a man
i think nobody really believes this storm can be anything

i have purple eye shadow! says Storm Eunice
she's going out tonight

i'm not
i'm both in and out always

of love

the wind has eaten through the fish and the railway sleepers
she's taken her toll on the train lines of Cambridge

Eunice bumps the blackbird who slept with me halfway up the road
sits next to me
bin bag? bus ticket? mind map from St Faith's? she offers me

i tell her, *i'm not that interested in the ways god meets the human*
she whistles
someone's dying today

—

capitalism thinks itself stupid
capitulum, the word for the head of a flower
derives from capitellum, meaning 'little head'

proof's in the roots of language

those who focus upon capitalism have heads like prunes, i say as we're
setting up the camera
we're taking a photoshoot with a disposable Eunice picked up on her
night out

the blackbird smiles
but i can't capture the scene because Eunice keeps panning me to a
side street
in which she has collected her treasures
through which she tries to be seen

—

'love too makes a man,' says Craig
who the fuck's Craig? asks Eunice
can you just be quiet for one moment please?

a whisper

'love too makes a man,' says Craig (i'm setting the scene)
and a swan, says Eunice

i exhale
don't harrumph in my ear!

the blackbird blinks

—

'love too makes a man,' says Craig (he'll want royalties at this rate)
of course it's men who are the ultimate symbols of fidelity and not the herring
gull — their squawk's unromantic to some ears

a perished tyre rolls by
takes with it the camera and the blackbird squawking

—

i'm almost sorry the lorry tipped over when Eunice stormed off
at least the pigeons will be eating tonight

'February's an interesting month
always changing its mind,' a friend once said on a bench before she
went to Greece

—

i feel like a weathervane
that has thrown itself off the roof

—

if i had a door, Eunice would be the kind of storm blowing in quietly
under the sill
she's back and she's upset but she's a strong lass
she's quietly dragging with her the pigeons
whose claws brought bark with them and yolk from their eggs
she won't talk to me
but the pigeons say plenty about what happened

i see a prison being built while out collecting snowdrops for Eunice
the pink torsos of the workers drop
down the sides of the walls
the prison casts a shadow over the state of the place

—

a drone flies over my head
like a red clot in a child's eye

—

Eunice's silence is the yellow daffodil opening its peeping eye
for the first time
it's too early to feed the bees, it's still cold
for the first time the children
searching for their mothers
return empty-handed

do you think truth matters today? i ask Eunice
she coughs
well, do you?
i'm not well! she turns on her side, whirling a dustbin into the sky

silence and stillness and the mist creeps in
it blocks the light
it makes my lips wet
my grip on Eunice is slipping

—

crashing echoing sounds
the trains are moving again

do you? i ask again in the middle of the night while Nature sleeps on a pile of torchwood
truth's a sliding concept these days, she says as breath slips through her now ossified lips

but aren't we post-truth in a post-modern age?
she's hardening to the reality of this

cinched in stone
she's gone

if Eunice could still speak i know what she'd say
that i'm wrong
that she doesn't much value fence posts and their boundaries

—

i lie down beside her even though she's gone
her father arrived to take her away to his garden, prop her up like a proper statue
set her in clay

i lie down beside her before she's lifted away
and place a snowdrop in her palm when Nature isn't looking

there's nothing mellow about the warmth of our yellow sun
or of my love

i can't wait to hold you
the way a storm holds a city

IIII

round me there are weeds and windborne infiltrators
from the polite gardens

such as the dandelion
its weapons lying underground

it takes more space than it needs so as not to waste
its competitive advantages
its leaves thicken round me while
it takes just a week to transform from a flower
into a puffball
ready to burst

—

i saw a woman strangling herself with a carrier bag
she couldn't carry on   i could: with her shopping

her blue face was like a love bite to me

i once had arithmetic friends
who equalled something else depending upon who they were with
but i gave up on maths as a kid
picked up the word
learnt it was a way to hide from an entire earth

but not the birds

—

i've just found out that Petits Filous isn't yoghurt
and that is my first realisation in a time of war

—

i feel powerless in front of this killing machine
tv screens surround my walk back to the bypass
i slap a tree
realise the way seeds pitter-patter round me is not comparable
to the mess of bombs dropping upon Ukraine

let's not pretend that brutality isn't best friends with civilisation
i would have cracked the woman's skull with a loose brick
for this cream-cheese-yoghurt pot
for a stick, if i were nest-building

—

i've started updating my feelings in places i know no one looks
i etch my name on a pavement below a skyscraper

i am
like the vertical and horizontal pages of a city
i am
thick with laden meaning
i am
and am not
at all like this city with its heady prunes walking around the
composition like dispirited mannequins

i want to kill myself, says Nature
same, it's easier to say

coiling ivy leaves up a lamppost
there's an odd colloquialism to suicide

i want to kill, myself, says Nature
instead of always dying

even the lamppost does not open its eye to witness a leaf fall to the
ground

—

there's never been a them and an us
only politics and political parties and   the people

and all people suffer
but not political parties

political parties have fun in times of war
there's nothing down about Downing Street

i know tragedy and tragedy is not a singular experience
we bear witness with the ancient silence of Eurydice to the heaps of
dead children

there's nothing different about being a voice of reason amongst a load
of shouting

so

i lick the pot of yoghurt dry
and i am moved by their sacrifice

—

there are no pigeons back at the bypass, no blackbird
they must be out searching for each other amongst the catalogues of
meaning i laid down for this city
searching for each other or for jam jars they'll get their heads stuck
in and feast until they starve

—

i'm as dedicated to the line
as a cokehead is

i'm feeling scripted into making meaning
it's better than being con-scripted to war i suppose

—

all the people
crying this morning

—

rapid-fire succession ballistic missiles highly dangerous
they upturn radiated sludge

they? where does the consciousness
of a missile lie?

i would be swiping right now through military videos if the birds
weren't calling me
they've found the blackbird hobbling away from some guy on a
motorway

—

'A highway is a way over which there exists a public right of passage,
that is to say a right for all Her Majesty's subjects at all seasons of
the year freely and at their will to pass and repass without let or
hindrance.' (*Halsbury's Laws*)

at what point does letting someone walk freely down one's road become a
colossal feat of presumption on the part of the crown? i ask Nature

silence

for which i have never cared
about which i scream like a deranged lunatic at the cars freely passing
the scene
of a homeless man and his pigeons and a mugger fighting over
a wrecked blackbird

i'm running with the blackbird at my chest
squawking as if to tell me to turn left
the bird was right, we should have turned left
but how could i have known what was right?
i have never flown over a city

—

i don't want my book to be thick enough to block a crack
under a door
i don't want to help you deny yourself any air

the pigeons could only distract the guy for so long
he catches up with us in the dead end of a street and bombards me
with punches like missiles at superhuman speed

he stops, he sees the bedsheets he could make out of the blackbird's
wing
he does not foresee the way such a bird might sing under the right
conditions

i try to stop him, then the waves
as my head collides with the concrete

—

i try to stop him, inform him that the energy content of wind is
proportional to its velocity cubed
and that i have a valuable friend who
that Eunice would have lit his face up with

there's not room for all of us in this city
me and the pigeons realise this as we scatter upon each other

the last thing i see is the blue and yellow tinge of their rheumy eyes
their flight like falling planes through the sky

—

if an animal gets out of control (this relates to my story, is clever, is
ethological)
then you've got to predict their movement through their preferred
environment in order to contain them
to all the animals out there, please listen to the blackbird telling you
to turn left

—

an example of packet loss: dead bird
in computer networking, IP over Avian Carriers (IPoAC) is a
proposal to carry internet protocol (IP) traffic by birds
when this happens, do you think the monarchy'll have to make a law
about the highways or flyovers of the sky?

i'm not depressed, i'm disenchanted
scuppered like a plebiscite before it's even been counted

—

i count the birds that are dead around me
bodies like crumpled blue cans

blood trickling into a storm drain
he took the blackbird with him

the library is the last free place i could go to wash off the blood
and ensure there will be silence while i observe my mourning

—

the muscled play of water on my face
is like the spasms of the still-dying birds

—

a cat precisely places its paws through the library
such assured stepping and not much lying
i find the library to be not much like
parliament and the rat race

i wander now lonely as a fucking cloud
i trip on a rock
face down i'm level with the world
i might not know a lot
but i know i'll find it, my blackbird
my blackbird

to

IIIII

here it gets difficult
to follow me
to follow me
i've split in two
the double as a time machine
for pathways from
and out of abuse

if it feels
right
why not?

—

i was sold once
on words i didn't understand

on fickle
liquid promises

i slipped the quid into the mechanism
turned the lock

it costs just one pound in this city to close a locker
but more like a million to own and close a door

i have a friend, not the one on the bench in Chania but another
who'll be on a bench this summer studying in Jordan for her Arabic

a friend who read to me a medieval lyric, called a lay
in which a woman looks at a hawk; in a single line it transforms into
a knight
this is 'the narrative gap of medieval transformation'
but the details are what contemporary cinematics shows so well

the lengthening of bird into man

—

the 'flexiseal' promise of the logo on my goggles
was enough to convince me that this was a logical purchase
because seals swim easily in water
just as readily on their backs as their bellies

the tint of the plastic blued my eyes
to our clumsiness in the water

the aviation division of Lloyds bank has lost over £600 million since
the Russian invasion
it seems the workers have become birdlike in their scattering

they stalk the banks for opportunity
they shag each other then duck out of the room

premise the meeting as a chat, same species as the bluethroat
they fly off when their manager's throat's turned blue

to the heights of
professionalism

—

freedom from, says Nature
as opposed to freedom to

i might have said the same a few days ago
that sometimes all we have are prepositions
that sometimes all we have are prepositions and not places
that sometimes all we have are prepositions and not places to go to

while i'm searching the bottom of a swimming pool
the person in the story crawls through dustbins in search of birds

—

i am not tired of narrative
but i am ignoring it like the emails from professionals who have
affronted me

it would not be contractually sound
for me to say abused

but it would be acceptable to my university for me to continue
meeting with someone who has

—

the way he liked me wet
when he poured the bottle over me

i was told 'it is *education* in the strictest sense'
by someone 'sorry to be all patriarchal and stuff'
'it is learning how to get on'
having these half-hour meetings with people who care about me
yet cannot quite admit
that outside of civilised society a different kind of meeting occurs
between concrete and hip
between concrete and flesh

i would not have taken it
in quite the same way
if i hadn't needed the approval of the committee

—

man lengthens
into demand

i am back to talking with Nature again
because all the birds are dead and gone, have left

we're at dinner picking over scraps of pigeon
i'll carry them with me somehow

what made you change your mind from just fucking to dating? i ask
you, says Nature

we're going out now
although i might still be fungible

in the pool i soak and expand like a shroom
someone'll pick to consume

i am mush
wedged like clay in between
the curling scrubland of
a lady's legs

and one man's face looks like it's collapsing
from its own gravitational pull

i have noticed none of us are in
proper working order

—

we are our own kind
of weathering

one total
social pecking order

a line
of sorts

that carves through and so levels
our valleys into

crumbling mounds down back alleys

what am i supposed to say when Nature realises that i walk on land
as clumsily as i swim

legs shaking after
him?

'here's an apple
that has nothing going for it' laughs a landowner, who Varda records
Agnès Varda, who is more natural than Nature, than the man who
privatises his land then tosses fruit around like he tosses people off
his land

i take the apple, eat it to the core
i have been feeling frayed lately

but am reminded that such a metaphor
means i never lost my

core, so i sling the remains of the apple at Nature's forehead
walk off with my own

it would be so easy for me to let myself fall below the water, listen to the sounds of people crying for a rubber float to be thrown my way but i continue with the breaststroke

there are so many of us sitting in this
we're going to need more benches
we're going to have to storm the council

i might finally be able to
sleep then

—

no one can glean a corpse
like family

family treat bodies like offerings
like vultures they snatch at day-old meat

i learnt yesterday that i keep secrets from people
and that has made lines all the easier

—

i look at my wrist
see the tag that says 333

i exit the pool and switch lockers
to the number 328

i am both myself and my mother
whose birthday number is 3, mine's 28

even though for months now she hasn't spoken to me
says i treat her like a number, like an ATM machine

but she is a much better swimmer than that
and me

bite it, says an imitation of Nature
no
now
fuck off before i rip your head off and shit down your neck, says Sweet Eve

bite the apple
it's a Granny Smith, it's too sour
tart!

Sweet Eve's ripped a branch from off the tree, tapped 'Nature' on
the head with it

for now i leave the pool
and eavesdrop on a conversation

'i don't know where Charlotte is'
'me neither'

me neither
except that Charlotte is because she has been
despite this
i think she could have been at the bottom of the pool

like and unlike a fish
they'll be reeling her body out of the reeds of her mother

out of the rubbish i reel a train ticket
hear a flapping sound overhead

it's for this afternoon
it's heading to the station

soon i'm flapping to the station
believing the sound to have been the blackbird

—

the human soul under pressure is
like the gull's gut

contorting itself around chips
and the royal head of our banknote-queen

that's what i call
a regal seagull

i somehow lost my card on the walk back to my college
i became visitor T417

i discover a note attached by the housekeeper on a pin board by a
closed window
it reads as it demands:

> *Dear Students*
> *The centre of Cambridge has a pigeon problem.*
> *This poses a health risk and we need to ensure that they do not get*
> *into the building.*
> [insert everywhere] *is a popular area for pigeons to roost.*
> *Please take care to ensure that gyp or corridor windows are not left*
> *open if areas are unattended for any length of time.*
>
> *Thank you.*
> *Ass(t.) Housekeeper*

i look at the note
am currently not a student of sorts

i whistle and leave
as a light breeze blesses the room

a station worker won't check my ticket won't let me through
tells me to off myself

now, birds are never insolent
so i off myself around the corner and scale the fence

my feathers protect me from barbed wire

i lie down
i straddle the fence

i swim and
i walk perfectly inadequate by some standards

i am the deviant of a storm and
i stand at the tracks as a spectator to birds circling overhead

it is lonely being at the centre of things so
i sit back, watch them fly

i cannot see the bird i was searching for
but there is the guy who i think captured it

IIIIII

i could apologise to a tree
for all this wasted space

say sorry in the title of my book
or i could say that

things exist
in air

—

like the dead bird on the tracks
it stinks out the hanging place

the guy laughs with a forked tongue
at the body pried open like a purse

there is its ticket-heart
its zip-flesh ripped open

the inside of a bird
is nothing short of manufactured these days

and there could very well be the photo of a family member
a lover lodged in a locket-bird alone

fat and lustreless is the eye of a camera
rotating above me

it stops on a lady with a handheld
a worker approaches her after a minute or two
'it is not legal to take a photo in a train station for commercial
purposes or with a tripod,' he says, pointing to the camera
'i'm just train-spotting,' she says, 'entirely personal use'

the man slinks away while
she takes another shot

i could spot at least three cameras
recording above me

i take half of the pool with me when i leave
head to the wall i hoist myself up and out
you could call it drowning
or a session tasting the finer things in life
the amount of old man's piss i've swallowed

my mother couldn't have known about the amount of phthalates she
consumed when she was pregnant with me
about the poison coating her medication to limit its effect on the
stomach

couldn't have known she was swimming like a fish
with plastic spilling out of its pulpy lips

—

spilling out from and back into
her own mother

such a death in the family left her
dead herself and drowsy

she would squint at the clock face
in a kitchen that has stayed the same since before the day i was born

—

there is a tonne of child
sandbagged around her waist

another friend another bench another space the council cannot force
us from
this time this friend is sitting having a picnic with her granddaughter
who is a flower
the iris flower the rainbow goddess the deliverer of messages and in
life of arrow signs as though she might shoot down all her coming
worries with her position
the iris flower and her sun-kissed cheeks, spitting grape seeds,
letting go of plates they shrug at the sunset
decide each other's faces are the thing worth watching

this friend tells me over the scratch of ice cubes in a glass
that waiting gets in the way of life

i watch the flowers lolling around a shrinking patch of grass

—

the felt-tip green of a butterfly flies by me
i feel like a child in a nursery

a pigeon appears with a match-lit eye
like a judge, an executioner
we're both waiting for an order that'll send us flocking

—

what is happening
is curdling everything too soon
even love

the pigeon flies at the approach of a train
shocked from its perch it swerves in the air and misses the guy

the pigeon flies away
i've missed my opportunity, i say

the guy steps onto the train
exquisite with his iron-breast

i have forfeited my leadership
it was not my bird, i think as i stumble forwards

towards the wicked lip of the track edge
it was not my blackbird not my

that bird's wood-slatted ribs
crushed by the train that hit it

i sat in a chapel the other night in my big gay coat
talking to a god whose answer is only sometimes no

no that was a lie
the house of god was closed the night i needed him
i sat outside on the granite steps of a fountain
happily pouring itself an eternal supply

—

i've drunk so much pool water that perhaps i've ingested Charlotte;
she left behind a set of muffled scrawls at the bottom of the pool,
some etchings of the underside of swimmers' feet as she fought to
breathe

—

like the underside of the train
so many take the time to slot themselves under

brake light
judder

—

the world did not become
a pit of char

a woman holds on to me
carries me all the way to a seat she had reserved for herself and for
no one else
but me

i'm sure you'll love me into shape
like that bird

IIIIIII

i bought a book called *In Parenthesis*
took the label, wrapped it round my pencil

(now i'm writing, in parenthesis,
with my in parenthesis pencil)

—

the lady doesn't look at me
and at first i don't dare speak

it's now or never
the book she's reading

as lots and lots of lamb and sheep
distantly munch grass

it's the fourth and last Sunday of Lent
it's the last day i could speak to my mother before it's just another
day

it's Mothering Sunday
currently neither of us have a mother
but we do have two rooms with four walls each
and the same surprising sweep of sky
whereunder my desk and her mantelpiece are lined with gifts that
remember our time together

painted elephant, cupped hands, golden car boot eye of Bast

i took one half of the clear-quartz tower when i left
left you the base
it split when you installed the camera, in case
the neighbours acted upon the death-threats

for years, i would place the two together
to keep from you, mother,
the fact of their separation

'let's not all fall out'
a lady sort of said to her train of children as they scrunched down
the aisle

and there was the father
this persistent fellow with backpacks and rucksacks
swaybacked under the weight of a kid clambering up his shoulders

the moisture in the air nearly
folded us all together

—

then there was Nature
ambling down the aisle
at me he smiles
tries to sit with us

he is denied by the swipe of a dug-out hand
the pink streams of time run across her crumpling skin

she looks up says to him, *i like my elbow-room*
oh right, Nature says not not cross
he sighs, finds a seat where he can keep an eye on me

there are two women behind me on the train
posh and proper

one proclaims, 'i felled a tree and Jesus wept!'
whatever that means

Nature shakes his head
i feel like i have to kill myself to be taken seriously

—

i heard a noise in the pool today
some glug-glug thrumming sound like a beluga whale
i think Charlotte's finished
with silence

—

swimming is a persuasive sport
if you stop, you'll drown

people move away from me
it's postural and entirely possible i curl into myself sometimes
resemble the sickle and the scythe
rather than the horseshoe
conjure up the death-tread of the hooves of the four horsemen
rather than the pure horsepower that drives the wheat from root

people move away from me
but not you, not you Una
you start speaking to me about how
happiness is no mystery

—

the world could do and do without i suppose
being a little more cuckoo

i went this weekend with my love to an exhibition called *Light Work*
at Cambridge Artworks
and if 'gardening is always an act of optimism'
'an action that believes in a future'
we could all plant a seed and grow a tree
collectively get going a wood, larger than some people's
shitty-city-worlds
one that'll continue itself for thousands of years
much longer than the place i visited
which has two more years on its tenancy

at night you can hear the scurry and the pratfalls
of mousy developers sniffing the place out

—

in spite of the overcast
the sky jitters
white

shadows provide a covering
for what's up-and-coming

a report announced the other day that seventeen out of twenty-two
healthy volunteers carried quantifiable amounts of microplastics in
their blood
they measured plastic particles as small as 700 nanometres, one
nanometre being equal to one billionth of a metre
perhaps it really is the small things in life that matter

i wonder how many birds still have berry-lined stomachs
we are fantastically plastic people

—

i don't have an oven or a hob in my student accommodation
so unless you can bake a cake with a kettle
i'm going to have to settle for baking a Simnel cake on the page
and send it to you, mother
in a letter, if you'll let me

i wonder can you list a life
or can you list alive?

Una's children, John, Daniel, and Laura
Daniel and Laura are twins
Laura does Hispanic Studies, Daniel did Maths, John works in commerce
she was there by mistake that day, had planned to stay with her
brother some miles away
she'll probably be in Edinburgh about now, two weeks away visiting
John
she is one of life's movers, a retired nurse
she goes sea-swimming in her coastal town in Ireland every day
she said it's addictive, the mattress that is the ocean
her husband is afraid of flying;
she don't give a fuck about that and goes on holiday anyway by herself
she sent 100 euros' worth of baby food and nappies to Ukraine,
which we know is worth much more than the value of euros
Una said that Jack is a very Irish name
and that she has family in America: New York, Washington,
Massachusetts
           i told her how i wish to see America one day
she has not seen her distant family for years
Una doesn't read as much as she wishes
she is afraid of war
she thinks Putin should be tried for war crimes
for Una it's not necessarily about the swimming, it's about the
calmness of being in water, it's about the repetitive motion,
swimming in the sea releases endorphins she tells me
           she's going grey like the cloud-closed sky
           despite this there are ginger streaks of daylight
           i sat with her from precisely 11:15–12:50 that day

Una told me to fuck everyone else's judgements off
she said it was nice to meet me and that she'd keep her eye out

i liked Una
and the image of her keeping her eye out

reminiscent of the full-looking moon
its lunar arrows firing down at the developers
who dart around all hotchpotch,
trying not to squeal, to make a sound that'll turn
the overlord head of a hunting night
owl

—

an arrow suicidal i swim
straight-backed i aim for the end of the pool
for the wall that is my safety

according to NYKT Marine Co., Ltd
'the number of pirate attacks has been sharply increasing'
'Jacklight's very strong light beam
works as a stern warning
to the pirates
and also helps
you with early
detection
of pirates'

apparently i'm a light, not a desk lamp but military-grade
with optimal characteristics close to that of a solar beam
and a powerful threatening effect
i'm supposedly compact and lightweight
with easy installation, but first you have to source electricity
still if you turn me on and look straight at me
i'll blind you

they seem careless, the little animals of the world, i say
is that why we envy them? asks Nature leaning forwards in his chair

they seem careless like children, i say as i think about the male tailor bird
born with a little yellow hard hat
aware its life will be a constant construction site
weaving its bauble home out of natural fibres
it dangles like spit, like a tear drop
that'll fall down your face when the wind blows

is that why we   a child throws a paper ball at Nature's head, rolls
back laughing

—

as they walked the country lanes as small gifts
children would gather violets and wildflowers
to take to their mother-church or give to their mothers

i ask Nature to search for the guy
this dove of a guy this demon
is too busy looking outside
at the dips and the heathland of his mother-planet
at the tracks that cut through her hips

she is impossibly silent to him

—

the weather was no accident to me
she descended upon this city
feral, ring-necked, pockmarked
a beauty ephemeral blasting
she wore no masks with me
except those of old age and asking

keep letting the day be massive
Eunice had said to me

the train passes a place called March
and, like the month, the trip is gone for another year

IIIIIIII

water does not hold on
it is too free for that

the force of my body is not remembered by the pool
but is made space for

—

the daylight on my wall
resembles the glass shallows of a riverbed

dearly
i'd hold them dearly
the disturbances
if i could get to them

i open my palm
black soot drops out
like the ripoff
of train wheels
touch me
and i'll blacken you

the underneath of the train sparks
some piles of stone as it slows

despite our show of levelling
the entrance to a city is an oddly crumbled place

—

myself am
a pile of bricks
only the premonition of a house

—

Nature will not face me
i have been sitting with him since Una departed at the previous stop

we're continuing
in silence
it seems passing a quarry has
mesmerised him

of course we bruise when someone hits us
violence leaves a trace like a debt

and not even the land can forgive
or entirely forget the grudge
of a war

—

i can see the guy, i say to Nature
who isn't paying attention so
i slap Nature on the hand
his dry look tells me this is something i'll have to do on my own

i hesitate   sit back down and wait those final juddering half-miles
we'll soon be arriving at the last stop today

juice of berry
sweet black tar clinging to the roof of someone's mouth
the cart is wheeled past me and Nature, who says he doesn't want
anything but is evidently parched

all the heat of this place and
we can't afford anything

wearily Nature calls the man pushing the cart, looks at me
it seems it's my turn to take care of him now
i pull a coin from my pocket
just 5p, the amount Rishi Sunak saved for me
and? what? what are all the things you can do with 5p?

it's easy to see why comedy shows struggle
it's hard to parody today

the worker looks away
he doesn't see how quickly i swipe to fill the ridges of my mouth

sorry nothing today, i say

piece of piece of biscuit ground by molars
Nature's tapping with such feverish litany
he covers the sounds i make as i regurgitate into his mouth

wildflower, sunflower
tomato plant
birds, bears, and the occasional
bigfoot

stymie them then stymie myth
stymie me this city

—

toss-up, the people are moving
they're heading for the exits

—

breath like woodsmoke
tinny sweat brought tears to my eyes
as i'm running, without Nature
after the guy

the pigeon was domesticated trained housed placed whatever you
want to say
then it left exited escaped
and instead of being named wild like it always was
we called it FERAL

a thing unwanted in any landscape

—

i lose the man
find the world and its improbability

could be
could be
could be

the great tit

i scan my surroundings
there he is

—

all there is
is air between us

begin

IIIIIIIII

the man turns, looks at me
Nature slowly steps down from the long curve of the train
we're all stiff-legged and thumbing for the line to take

—

the splash and gurgle of footsoles
the almost-chorus of knees
shins fists scuffling   (no one's paying us attention)

a train pants
          out the station

it takes the whole of me not to fall
into action

a truckload of plastic enters our oceans
every minute

we faith the world like Pascal's automaton

Pascal's automaton refers to a passive believer
active faith is not always possible, is not pragmatic, is too draining
you place faith on the back-burner
knowing you'll be able to again
part memory, part prediction

then you wake up with your back burnt

they say skin renews fortnightly
that it's thinnest at the eye and
thickest in my mind, but
dead skin like dead men
is clingy; it's hard to rip meat
from the bone

soon though   *you won't have touched me*

disturbance quarrel brawl and bash-away
all synonyms for fisticuffs

at first i can't think of synonyms for the handcuffs the security
guards brought out
but then restraint
wristlets gyves even snips
the guy slips from the platform

eyes closed, i'm fighting the air

i collide with Nature
some old guy who stinks: he's trying
to remember where he was heading

first, a narrative of trying
for an older generation:

draw your sword sir
no you draw your sword sir
you first sir
no you first sir
my dear sir
dear sir?
i'm going to poke my sword in you sir
oh dear
oh
sir

[enter the twenty-first century theatrical hall of mirrors]

you man movin bookey?
why you wylin?
whip out your shank then
dickhead ting, fighting ting

[on the flipside of the mirrors]

in common business parlance the asset that is the bird
WHACK
Sweet Eve's had *enuf*
she's bringing back paradise

some responsibly wack scientists in the Proceedings of the National
Academy of Sciences (PNAS)
i'm glad some people are proceeding, are moving forwards despite the times
despite there being only 26/650 MPs with a science degree in 2015,
despite then at the general election in 2019 (the requirements having
changed to only an 'interest' in a STEM subject) there being only
103/650 MPs
'interest' is an interesting word in a proof-driven society, both flat
and financial
it scales up like inflation into an overpriced democracy
why are basic necessities sold at luxury prices?

        (shut up words shut up facts)

some responsibly wack scientist in 2015, Corey Callaghan and his
Everglades marsh trip: he sees tree swallows
        (fuck sake words fuck sake birds)
he and two other researchers from Sydney estimate there are likely
between 50 billion and 428 billion birds on earth
        (how many words are there?
        what about all the streamed music constantly pouring
        through my window?
        can you tell i'm stressed?)

i think being free
must be being alone

despite this and the scientists
50 billion+ birds to 8 billion people
my thoughts aren't very specific

man is
gone

how will i
find my bird?

—

bark is a defensive layer on a tree
my mother's face was wood-grey when i last saw her
before i saw her leafing like a tree
shedding its summer canopy

page 84 of a bird book my friend gave me
the nightjar, describes Edmund Sandars:

> *Manners: Sits on ground during day* [same]. *Suffers much from*
> *parasites. Dust bather. Returns to same spot yearly* [pain?]. *Cock*
> *arrives first. In courtship, wags tail like a dog and flies, smacking*
> *wings together above back. Feigns injury to decoy from eggs or young.*
> *Has favourite trees and perches lengthwise on bough. Hunts only after*
> *dark.*

Nightjar's also a cocktail bar in London
so is a place called Embargo Republica (has 'pub' and 'bar' in, clever)
there is no ban on what you can make
and in this place they create me

Candyjack cocktail
fresh, fruity, balanced?
Jack Daniel's, raspberry purée, cranberry juice, gomme, fresh
lemon, mint, lollipop

i imagine, although i have yet to sip myself
i sit deep in an airless part of the gut

all are narratives of trying
alcoholism and flying
some jug-jugs passing overhead

in Anthony Tubbs and Andre Nussenzweig's paper 'Endogenous DNA Damage as a Source of Genomic Instability in Cancer' they write:

it has been estimated that each human cell is subject to approximately 70,000 lesions per day

our whole body is a narrative of trying
but i'm not sure we manage to regenerate faster than we fall apart

sometimes i find the burden of feeling and thought to be too much
it's a good job language, like water, bends to us
like wet plaster

the UN is a very suspicious narrative of ''''''''''''''''''''''trying

just know that the people felt for you
even if the politics didn't

love creates
inebriate rot

that scrambling plant
that desperate hook-on

a shot of 200–250 million spermy fuckers
only 200 make it to the egg
none but one inside the egg, the ordinary rest die by acidic fluids

fuck me, i fuck you and your pussy's a slaughterhouse
it's not easy being born

—

and when it feels like everything in life is conspiring against you
i hope this helps
you rise

foamy bubbling rise
    click
goes the kettle i'm boiling pasta in because it's even difficult cooking
fusilli in this hobless college

i wonder
because we're all so close to each other in this city
if, in terms of matter, we are one solid?

vibrant rubbings, lights turn on/off
people living opposite the train tracks can't decide whether or not
they want to see each other tonight

—

i haven't got a clue
thinks the average man

as Nature stands there helplessly staring
asking: *what to do?*

—

like feathers
our delicate white failings

i give up
with trying

IIIIIIIII

as per Article 17 of the GDPR, right to erasure,
right to be forgotten   i
am requesting you erase all of my personal data within thirty days
please notify me once my data has been successfully erased by
replying to this

warmest wishes
some form of permanently exhausted pigeon

[outside a statuary]

you have to move or they'll take you
you have to go
i don't want to leave you
you have to
otherwise they'll take you
you have to go
i won't be apart from you
then listen, because otherwise we'll spend the rest of our lives kept apart by
walls
my perfect outlier
please listen, because you have to go knowing nothing holds us apart so long
as we keep moving; it's mobility that's contemporary; i'll lap the earth until i
see you, the horizon, again
the space that's never our own
the space where sky relives the sea

i collided with Nature
now he just looks at me
fits between my body and the floor that's chalked with the yellow
outlines of man and woman indicating where traingoers should stand

to relieve the hurry of pain
he chews the cud of his cheeks, he's mute
cause it never will be the same
once said or thought
or so i thought until that casual slip
from me:

Nature stood up
left the station and me with
a slant in the movement of his eye
as though he remembered
the thrill of the river
runs through to the brick

a squirrel leans on a fence
poised like a sandy question mark

the urge to clap my hands at it
is strong

silver
the handcuffs
like bracelets
except invidious
and tarnished
like a damaged beak

i became two moving feet
up the stairs and under the barriers

then you
standing in front of me on a dark side street

the high-pitched squeak of new trainers
that slight private fret in your eye

some beautiful man and

the subtlety of just encountering you

you were on my
mind all night

the way a needle holds an addict
the trace of dots up an arm
or how the buttercup blots of late spring lean
into one another

—

i felt the full-throated re-
lease of summer's green
bloom inside me
when i tried to speak to you

a line of pigeons adjusted
themselves along a telephone wire

their monotonous cooing
a familiar sound

their buffy-pink plumage
my breast

which i imagined you laid your head upon
instead you sauntered away

—

you were on my
mind all my life

i couldn't sleep by the switchyard
without the relief of wrapping round you
like the nearby wisteria
cradling itself

—

a ruptured drain speaks
keeps me up all night

darts, acid-green through the trees
the 25,000 escaped parakeets of London, now beyond
insist on living despite scientists' attempts to cull them

they're invasive
they threaten our crops
they've passed diseases on to humans

despite this
and our fend-for-yourself government's plan to delete   *only*
300 people each year
by sending asylum seekers 4,000 miles away to Rwanda

the stone passes through the gut of the bird
and it hungers again

you have to move or they'll take you
you have to go

i don't want to leave

—

there's a need in me to stay
awake, to be in the world

it's up to my GP if she wants to call it
insomnia

either way
i like the bare air
i like the slated-grey sky
and the harmonica-line of trees
whistling, their night-long whistling
all for me

a lone bird lands by me
shadowed by the purple
totem poles of the switchyard

it can't stay for long
it's on its way to Scotland from Senegal

it asks me how i am
i ask it how it is

different places, same sleeplessness
we both seem to say

that's the issue when food's inaccessible
and danger's inevitable
on the mind all night
you have to move
you have to go

the year-old osprey flies away with a ruffled salute
in the direction it just knows to take

'The pensive man . . . He sees the eagle float
For which the intricate Alps are a single nest,' writes Wallace Stevens
in a gorgeous poem

it's lovely and it's fine because poems aren't
life

otherwise
you'd have a pensive man wondering
and an eagle who looks down and sees in that singularity
dinner

a nearby giggle in a bush
green shiftings

and a park
full of eyeballs
watching

such possibility
in the dark blue of night

IIIIIIIIII

so blue
it's so blue
the water
we huddled onto a boat say hi to the waves
so bloody blue
someone fell in   *are you okay?*
panic cause
someone's drowning
so blue sea-bones sea-weeds sea-like-see-us-all-on-the-sea-floor
except for the yellow-boat-canary-float-tips-up
the waves sea-sawing-us
this glimpse of us above and
below the watershine
like confetti thrown
over our corpses

so blue
so bloody blue

the letters i type
look like pigeons' feet
across but more like within
my dark screen

i get up and leave the switchyard, walk through the park at night
but it's nearly day there's this great rusted gate at the end of a
lane in which the remaining moonlight shows me something of a
greater light: i see beauty in its dynamic objectivity writing on the
collapse of a wing the extension of the thing all-governing not just
compensatory for the windlessness but much more like sidling up to
us as a parent does holding our arms up as we learn to walk

moonlight being masterful these days
over the relatively tidal mind
forms a quiver
before truth
and goodness

i had no idea what to do
i managed a flat for a while
before i was forced to leave
for throwing a TV out of the window
among a number of other things
but nothing like first degree
murder; i am nothing
like the corporations running things
these days; there was a prison
near my flat, constructed right outside
of that dilapidated primary school;
it cancels out the optimism
of the colourful classroom
alphabet-boards; the featheriness
of unwalked grass, which of course
we've now trodden down; are we
content with only making
content these days?

the swifts are back
they fly tensed all the time like their shoulders are shrugged up

in the gardens
a bumblebee grumbles by me
a bursting up of flowers
over and over again and everywhere
leans as if great hands spin the world
back and forth
a fly bounces by me
i have never heard or never noticed
how sometimes they sound as happy as a trumpeter

—

a trumpeter, being a person who plays a trumpet
not what Google search results brought up first
Trumpeter, a company in China that manufactures plastic injection-
moulded scale model kits
          (try saying that without pulpy lips)
people collect models of planes, warships, unified ballistic missile
systems

whereas i sit too poor for all this
with the world just as it is

i am a fan
of the simple hereness of things

like water

—

so
blue
is the water dispenser locked behind two wooden doors in the
community centre
it is the only place not entirely closed this early in the morning

i sit in a waiting area in front of the reception, divided from me by a
sheet of glass
there is no one but me
and it doesn't exactly look like a place one could ask
for a cup of tea

i went this week with my love to Ickworth House
a building (with two wings) in which a guide responded via scripts

GUIDE: *let me impart my knowledge of a room i! spend my whole life in
    — wait?*

[on comes someone from the audience for a bit of audience
participation]

TEENAGER: *can anyone read these books?*
GUIDE: *no! not except under extremely exceptional circumstances*
TEENAGER: *what like climate change, war, end of the world forest-fire
    burning, birds falling from the sky in India, giant meteorites yearning to
    slam into us because of gravity; we really drag these things upon ourselves,
    don't we?*

[Guide stands a bit dazed]

TEENAGER: *how come all of these books are locked away?*
GUIDE: *conservation value*
TEENAGER: *huh?*
GUIDE: *CONSERVATION VALUE*
                [card reader beeps; embarrassed, the Guide tries to
                hide the machine]
TEENAGER: *it's a shame isn't it that if a library contains a world of
    knowledge*
GUIDE: *IT'S TO RESERVE I MEAN TO PRESERVE*
TEENAGER: *and we keep it closed, then what does that mean about our
    society? cause it seems to me the world'll get smaller that way*

GUIDE: *it's so the future generations can enjoy these books*
TEENAGER: *but i'm part of the next generation, i am our future*
GUIDE: *for the generations to come*
  LET'S HAVE A CONVERSATION WHERE EVERYTHING IS ONE WAY —
  i wasn't supposed to say that

[stand up]

SOMEONE FROM THE AUDIENCE: *the family who lived in this house*
  always used this library; they wrote in all the books and they shared them
  with each other, but now all their interpretations are just locked away?
GUIDE: *i'm sure you can find these books online*　　　　[stepping back]
SOMEONE FROM THE AUDIENCE: *but you're equating book with*
  content and neglecting the material 'value' of the book itself, which is
  inherent actually to the point of their conservation; it's whether or not you
  think it would be valuable to interact with the actual object that is a book,
  as opposed to a digitised version of the text in a different material setting?

[Guide sits, dazed]

FROM THE AUDIENCE: *in fact, what does that mean for us? are we*
  being made to be content these days enjoying nothing of our own material
  conditions and labouring for the supply of a generation supposedly latent
  within us?

[silence]

TEENAGER: *excuse me*   [the teenager taps the man on the shoulder]
GUIDE: *y-yes?*
TEENAGER: *i can see your card reader again*   [points to the guide's arse]

[he quickly turns to hide it]
[behind him a crowd of people like a fist]

the first thing i realise is
how much of a commodity electricity is
even the plug sockets have covers on in this
communal edifice

—

you can tap
a tree

it'll give

in zoology, the dove versus hawk strategy refers to competition
between two birds known as an actor and an opponent:
a 'hawk' attacks, while a 'dove' displays/retreats when attacked
it wouldn't be advantageous if both were a 'hawk', because both
could die fighting or be seriously injured without a substantial
'payoff'
neither would it be advantageous if both individuals were a 'dove',
because there would be so much time and expense wasted on their
displaying behaviour
meaning, in both examples, there wouldn't be a net gain but a
net loss, and following this insofar as a zoological model can be
superimposed upon 'human' behavioural patterns
survival depends upon a winner and a loser

the pattern on my pencil is of Picasso's doves of peace
they wonder as they write:
what do you think of the government's displays of peace?

a man enters the community centre and at first he doesn't see me
goes about his business
picking up a sign, he stumblingly places it two feet away
he is shocked by me or my big gay coat
or me in my big gay coat;
i have come to realise i am not dressed much for subterfuge

'what arrrrrr you doing here?' he asks like a pirate unacquainted
with the waves
hi there, i say with a bright-light smile
his teeth, black spots, far from the white bubbles you find on the
underside of water
and he doesn't smile

'are you here for the event this afternoon?' he asks
unfortunately not, i say
'you're not here for the ballet?'
no, but we can dance, what d'you say?
for a moment he looks at me then lifts his peg-leg up, 'not much of a
dancer these days,' he says
how'd you do that?
'drinking so much tea i got chronic gout'
can i have a cup of tea, please?
'you want gout?'
no but
'so if you don't want gout and you're not here for the ballet, what do
you want?'
i have nowhere else to go
'what, you're homeless?'
yeah, essentially
'oh right'   and he continues on with his life

he types in the key code to the door, lets it swing shut
i stop it with my foot

—

i look at the bodies in the water
they could be ice-bits
or plastic or white drifts of fluff
and dust floating around in it
i'm not sure

—

i drink the water so quick
i feel the swell of a tideline in my throat

at least i think it wasn't my fault
how the water dispenser tipped
i'm sure the carpet's floral pattern appreciated it, i say to the pirate who is
so angry everything he says slurs into a single rrrrrrrrrr

as he throws me out the building he shouts
'you can't be here!'

not very fucking community friendly then, is it? i say
then leave

you could see soaked
the underlying structures of the place
the wet rot of wood

i am trying not to let this world harden me
into stone

—

Schönlaterngasse, in central Vienna, was a street with a lovely
lantern that someone removed and put in a museum;
there remains though this 1577 myth, etched into the stone housing
in 1932, about a basilisk and a baker's apprentice

on the morning of 1212 a child, perhaps also twelve, noticed the
monster and before it could turn him and everyone else to stone,
he held a mirror up to it

the basilisk exploded, the lantern was taken and put behind glass, but
this place still tells the story of a kid who saved his neighbourhood

and people pass by it every day, some without even looking
stonefaced

i stare at some
crazy sunrise

the smell and swell
of brine underneath

a yellow and red
and lurid purple sky

i had not noticed before
how dynamic

a coastline is
in the morning

—

there's even a class divide
between suicides

a blue tit nipping
and nicking the inside of a planter

the notion of what
a bird does anyway

IIIIIIIIIII

i was born a storm

Oratia (Tora in Norway) was a European windstorm
who blew from the 28th–30th of October 2000

i arrived on her first day
my mother-storm told me that, as they opened, pure cyan-lines ran
lightning-effects through my eyes
and that to wreck the way the world is
i would become a proposition for the sky
instead of one of its pillars

what are you still doing here? asks Nature in his statuary, his garden
i could say the same for you, says Eunice in position
you better be moving
i can't and anyway i'd be too late, you were right all along
oh fuck that let's go
why?

      he laughs
sometimes why's too much to ask in the time you have
     you need to move
         you need to go past the disinterested backs of the statues, past
the whirring fringes of marram grass, past the breakers and the cynical regard
of the beachgoers carved too flat for you

a vatic tweet as guide: a bird appears singing
a battle-cry like a lovesong

the snowdrop falls from her palm
i can move, Eunice says facing the great arc of the morning

     —

the way a storm gets up one day
and just blows your garden away

it's curious to me how the word refugee is one vowel more than
refuge
and really close to refuse

that 'ee' sound, that frightened squeak
of a parliamentary mouse

—

the last orchid
petals-down
it throws itself off
to make room
for new connections

—

every time i held you i wanted to hug you so tight
you went inside of me

i walk towards the ocean
no bird, no company, no own room
there's open sewage along the road
spilling from a bright purple pipeline
besides marsh rosemary/sea lavender
its leaves like fingers wipe up the waste
not yet greyed but deeply green
its flourish

—

the inside of an orchid flower
resembles the inside of the mouth of a bird

—

why do you think i hugged you so tightly
it cracked your back?

a dead fish
and smoothed pebbles
form a storm beach
at the head

i reach the thin
crust of sand
thickening these quilted flats
stiffening as i walk

newly washed
by the distant
incoherent spume
of the sea

such disquiet
in me the cold air
envelopes the entirety
of my lungs like a pool

insubstantial
as if cut from paper
life in the mysterious cries
of the seagulls

a storm rummages above
a person looks at me, eyes like dead wood

—

i begin to feel
my body rock

—

the water whispers
sweet nothings to me

the waves between
these wooden groins
carry me
lightly

out

—

for the first time today in the pool
the fog of my goggles lifts

a light
in my mind
like a silk covering

i found a voice
in it

—

every time i enter the water
i make the decision to rely upon myself

it's like every single word is itself a love-act
letter-to-letter a correspondence, a relationship
as painted by Botticelli, when Venus rises from the waves, look and
see the formation of a word
there's love in the middle, or significance, meaning around which
the figures come together transported by a kind of gravity; they
the forces cover with clothing and dressings her love-significance-
meaning, as if this represents the adornment of the actual into
language from out of mystery and back into
like lips closing around a carnal lake is love dead, imperfect, or at
the very least not just a received idea but a distraction of wings in all
directions disparately brushing up against one another, sand in places
it shouldn't be but is, love like a room without much room, that
bruising, wild unrest
a space that's ours; part of the moanings of a caressing sea
and the bed of a shell
held up upon the glass italics of the waves

—

above me
the nerves of Eunice
fire through the sky
like hands reaching

187

underneath an unguessable forest
held in sleep

—

amongst the possibilities of the surf
waves wash over me

then comes colour

—

i'll never let you go
i don't mean having
i mean holding
i mean white lightning firing from the bloody above
i mean everything
between lightning my love and life
described in the shapes of clouds crossing a miraculous sky

the sea was grey like i'd been folded in sculptor's clay

and that first bird, that blackbird
held by the wind and searching
it flies to the horizon

notes

Each section was written under an accompanying title:

Poem
A nother Po*em*
my po*em*
Poem?
Po -   -   - *em*
p   o   *e*   *m*
po|*em*
p ~ *o* ~ *e m*
Poh?em
~~POEM~~
[Po*em*]
]   Poem   [

Towards a blackbird:

'My own friends are blackbirds', Katerina Gogou.
'Thirteen Ways of Looking at a Blackbird', Wallace Stevens.
'Quartier Libre', Jacques Prévert.
'Adlestrop', Edward Thomas.
'Mad Girl's Love Song', Sylvia Plath.

There was a muddy hole, behind my house. And birds.
A break from the backdrop. They dug me out at fifteen.

p. 11 *Ghosh writes about writers mining their own personal experiences for their work*, see Part 1, 'Stories' for an account regarding the threat of our indifference: Amitav Ghosh, *The Great Derangement: Climate Change and the Unthinkable* (London: The University of Chicago Press, 2016).

p. 19 *every breath you / take*, song by The Police.

They'll be watching you . . .

p. 21 *our faith in the stability of the stars remained unshaken / until 1572*, Tycho's Supernova showed the West the possibility for the 'fixed stars' to change.

Look up to the stars, then, involve yourself
in what they do.

p. 22 *to their surprise, they found pronounced dips in light*
https://www.ucl.ac.uk/news/2022/feb/planetary-bodies-observed-first-time-habitable-zone-dead-star (Accessed 19/01/2023).

p. 48 *i slap a tree*, read Tommy Pico, *Nature Poem* (Oregon: Tin House, 2017).

> *For the book that would not let me close*
> *but open.*

p. 53 *'A highway is a way over which'*, *Halsbury's Laws of England*, *Highways*, vol. 55 (2019), paras 1–91.

p. 59 *i wander now lonely as a fucking cloud*, a play on the first line of the poem 'I Wandered Lonely as a Cloud', in William Wordsworth, *The Major Works* (Oxford: Oxford University Press, 2008), pp. 303–304.

p. 67 *a friend who read to me a medieval lyric, called a lay*, the story 'Yonec' was read to me by Susanna Mackay, always wonderfully radiant. From *Lais de Marie de France*, ed. Laurence Harf-Lancner (Paris: Livre de Poche, 1990), pp. 182-209 (see specifically ll. 114–119).

p. 68 *that sometimes all we have are prepositions*, listen to: 'Too Many Birds', Bill Callahan.

> *We need*
> *We need more*
> *We need more birds*
> *We need more birds like*
> *We need more birds like heartbeats*

p. 74 *'here's an apple'*, from Agnès Varda's 2000 documentary *The Gleaners and I*. The way the landowner inflicts suffering upon people by giving just enough is similar to today's government. You might guess their slogan: *An apple a day keeps the beggars at bay.*

p. 78 *fuck off before i rip your head off and shit down your neck, says Sweet Eve* 'And to do that to birds was why she came', Robert Frost.

p. 81 *gyp*, at the University of Cambridge, gyp is used for a variant of a kitchen that includes, essentially, nothing that could support life.

p. 87 *say sorry in the title of my book* references Eileen Myles's beauty of a book, *Sorry, Tree* (Washington: Wave Books, 2007).

> *When reading this, I felt like I was free-falling.*

p. 92 *arrow signs as though she might shoot down all her coming worries with her position*

> *Make an arrow with your body. Position yourself*
> *in the wish of the stance.*
> *Akarna Dhanurasana.*
> *Kids don't sit still.*

p. 101 *i bought a book called* In Parenthesis references David Jones's *In Parenthesis* (1937).

p. 101 *it's now or never* references Lynda Page's *Now or Never* (2000).

p. 106 *and if 'gardening is always an act of optimism'*, artist's film by Sarah Wood – *Perennial* (2022): https://vimeo.com/687654603/fc986b767b

See also Sarah Wood (sarahwoodworld.com)

> *Glass butterfly.*
> *It's ornamental.*
> *It's unable.*
> *It relies upon something else to pick it up*
> *from off the shelf*
> *and convey it to someplace else. Wind*
> *like film.*

p. 107 *a report announced the other day*, Leslie, Heather A., et al., 'Discovery and quantification of plastic particle pollution in human blood.' *Environment International*, vol. 163, (2022) p. 107199.

p. 110 *according to NYKT Marine Co., Ltd*: https://www.nyktmarine.com/en/service/original/jacklight.php (Accessed 19/01/2023).

p. 130 *we faith the world like Pascal's automaton*, see fragment 252, 'we are as much automaton as mind', in Blaise Pascal, *Pensées* (London: Penguin Books, 1995), pp. 247–248.

p. 133 *dickhead ting, fighting ting*, listen to Skepta's 'Crime Riddim'.

you could also listen to MadMax and NitoNB's 'Drilling'.

p. 134 *wack* to be clear is a familiar term of address in certain areas of England.

p. 134 *despite there being only 26/650 MPs with a science degree in 2015*, Information shared to me via a friend, Jessica Gill, who attended a lecture in which this data was presented.

p. 134 *he and two other researchers from Sydney*, Callaghan, Corey T., Nakagawa Shinichi., Cornwell, William K., 'Global abundance estimates for 9,700 bird species', *PNAS*, vol. 118, no. 21 (2021), p.e2023170118.

p. 136 *the nightjar*, as appears in the third edition of Edmund Sandars, *A Bird Book for the Pocket* (London: Oxford University Press, 1933), p. 84.

p. 137 Tubbs, Anthony, Nussenzweig, Andre., 'Endogenous DNA Damage as a Source of Genomic Instability in Cancer', *Cell*, vol. 168, no. 4 (2017), pp. 644–656.

p. 156 '*The pensive man*', read 'Connoisseur of Chaos' in Wallace Stevens, *The Collected Poems of Wallace Stevens* (New York: Vintage Books, 2015) pp. 228–229.

p. 170 *in zoology, the dove versus hawk strategy*, Smith, John M., 'Evolutionary Game Theory' *Physica D: Nonlinear Phenomena*, vol. 22, no 1 (1986), pp. 43–49.

p. 174 *Schönlaterngasse* (most accurately rendered in English as Lovely Lantern Alley)

p. 182 *no own room* references Virginia Woolf's *A Room of One's Own* (1929).

p. 186 *a light* see Dante, *Paradiso*, translated by Allen Mandelbaum (Berkeley: University of California Press, 1982) p. 296 (ll. 139-141):

> and my own wings were far too weak for that.
> But then my mind was struck by light that flashed
> and, with this light, received what it had asked.

I think it must be all love.

Acknowledgements

I'm writing this a year on from when I started *Enter The Water*. The birds are returning. Yesterday, the intrusion of a magpie in what is no longer *my* house but *ours* was a worryingly welcome event. The magpie is back on the fence now, preening. In that way now is a good time to acknowledge. My first is to the natural world. Its old and unexpected pleasures. I am reminded how life comes back again and will continue to do so if we care about it, hopefully even if we don't.

The public good that are natural spaces, neither exclusive, nor hostile, were a retreat of mine. Somewhere I could sit, for free, feeling the generosity of the sun. I liked them. Grantchester meadows and the river walkers of the Cam. I was borne along by it.

Our world then. To it, all my love.

And all my love to the people who gave me their time. Heart-power. Ali Smith. Liz Mayne. Bhanu Kapil. Sasha Dugdale. John Gallas. Kit de Waal and Kim Squirrell. Ian Patterson. Denise Riley, for the courage. Tracy Bohan. Sarah Castleton and the team at Corsair.

To the artist who designed the book's cover. Thank you, Simmon, for the celebration of colours. Fireworks.

To my beloved others. My mother. Dawn. Sarah. Jess and Jess. Kieran. Susanna. Kaleigh. Lidija. Macy. Lewis. Buddy.

The blackbird. The pigeons.

Every which way and where.

Again, my love. As much of it as I can manage.